Goblins

By Jennifer Guess McKerley

KIDHAVEN PRESS

An imprint of Thomson Gale, a part of The Thomson Corporation

THOMSON

GALE

Detroit • New York • San Francisco • San Diego
New Haven, Conn. • Waterville, Maine • London • Munich

For more information, contact
KidHaven Press
27500 Drake Rd.
Farmington Hills, MI 48331-3535
Or you can visit our Internet site at http://www.gale.com

LIBRARY OF CONGRESS CATALOGING-IN-PUBLICATION DATA

McKerley, Jennifer Guess.
  Goblins / by Jennifer Guess McKerley.
    p. cm. — (Monsters)
  Includes bibliographical references and index.
  ISBN 0-7377-3530-9 (hard cover : alk. paper) 1. Goblins. I. Title. II. Monsters
(KidHaven Press)
  GR549.M37 2006
  398'.45—dc22
<div align="right">2006001261</div>

CONTENTS

CHAPTER 1

Legendary Creatures

In 1830 people on the southern coast of England warned travelers to beware. They told a story about a peasant who walked to town in the dark. He was not sure which path to take, but soon he noticed a light ahead. It came from a lantern held high by a small, dusky figure that led the way. The peasant thought the person with the light knew the right direction, so he followed. Suddenly he almost slipped off the edge of a high cliff. He grabbed onto a bush and barely stopped himself from plunging into the raging water below. Then he saw it was a goblin that held the lantern. Its monstrous face broke into a loud, cruel laugh as it hovered in midair over the gorge. The goblin blew out the candle in the lantern and disappeared.

One of the goblin's favorite acts of mischief is to use his lantern to lure unsuspecting travelers to a cliff's edge or some other dangerous place.

Goblin stories like this one were told as fact all over Europe during the 19th century. At that time, many people thought the beings were real. Goblins are imaginary magical creatures, yet almost every culture on Earth once had a tradition of believing they actually existed. Long ago, uneducated people used **superstitions** to explain events they did not understand. They blamed mythical beings like goblins for death, crop failures, fires, and earthquakes, as well as other natural disasters.

Countless goblin tales come from all over the world. The stories give various descriptions of goblins, but the creatures are always evil. One of the earliest accounts is about the horrifying goblin spider from Japan. According to the myth, any spider seen at night is a goblin and must be killed immediately. If left alive, the spider grows to a gigantic size. Its huge eyes flash, and its fanglike teeth drool as it stalks people and traps them in a web of terror. The legendary mountain goblins from Japan are also brutal. Part man and part bird, these winged creatures drive people to madness and hurl them from the sky.

UGLY, FRIGHTFUL SPIRITS

The goblins of British and American folklore are just as spiteful as Japanese ones, but their appearance differs greatly. They look like hideous, shrunken humans. These goblins delight in appearing out of nowhere. In a typical encounter, the stunted creature waits quietly, ready to pounce. Its **grotesque**

face scowls. Its dark, cruel eyes glare. Gnarled, claw-like fingers hang from its misshapen arms and body. Soon the human gags at the filthy odor and turns around. In a flash, the goblin springs. Its ghastly face presses close, eyeball-to-eyeball with the person. As the human shrieks with terror, the satisfied goblin cackles and vanishes into thin air.

In this Japanese illustration, a samurai warrior fights off a group of hideous winged mountain goblins.

An Irish goblin known as the Cold Lad of Hylton dances with malicious glee after a family gives him warm clothes.

Goblins are mean, clever spirits with **unearthly** powers. They have the ability to fly and are not bound as humans are by the limits of time, space, and gravity. They never grow old, and they live for thousands of years. Although they normally stand only 1 to 2 feet (0.3 to 0.6m) tall, their size changes when they **shape-shift** into the forms of people and animals. They use such powers to shock and surprise, just as they alarm humans with their ability to suddenly become visible or invisible.

Traditionally, goblins appear as creatures with brown or copper-colored skin. Sometimes they are hairy and sometimes they have tails, but they always have horrid breath. They are said to hate humans, but they wear clothes to mimic them. Usually their attire is green, black, or brown. Goblins also wear pointed caps above their pointed ears and bulging eyes. According to **Celtic** tradition, goblins began hating people in ancient times.

Underground Creatures

Celtic legend states that goblins once lived far below Earth's surface, so people did not know about them. The creatures used shovels to dig for silver and gold that they saved. Sometimes they raided **gnome** colonies and stole their stockpiles of these valuable metals.

A woman shares a bounty of magical fruit with goblins that have shape-shifted into various animals.

Three grotesque goblins share a drink as they seek shelter from the daylight in a dank and sunless room.

Everything changed when humans began to mine Earth. As people dug deeper, they got too close to goblin dwellings. Eventually, the mining destroyed the goblin settlements. Most of the beings came to the surface, where their distorted bodies were more suited for darkness than daylight.

Some goblins sought shelter in gloomy places like caves, under rocks, and the roots of trees.

Others settled in hidden parts of forests, swamps, and wild mountain regions. Furious at humans, the goblin race swore **revenge**.

The few goblins that stayed underground caused deadly accidents and fires in mines. Those who lived above ground roamed about and tormented people. Tales were told about hunters, lumberjacks, fishermen, and travelers who met danger in the woods and on the road. It was reported that goblins kidnapped people and enslaved them in a magical realm. If these people returned to the human world, they became crazy. Soon they crumbled into piles of ashes.

Tormenting Humans

Eventually goblins moved closer to their enemies. They chose farms to take over and households to rule. Each goblin staked out its own **territory** and would not tolerate the presence of another spirit. Goblins also tried to scare away the stronger humans who threatened their control over weak **mortals**. Goblins especially disliked ministers because of their good influence on people. They also hated those who prayed often and those who did not drink liquor.

Sometimes goblins worked together to cause the death of a human who opposed them. The group would stay invisible until they passed the human they wanted to frighten. Then only that person could see them as they carried a coffin in a funeral procession.

The human also saw himself or herself dead in the coffin. He or she then collapsed and soon died from shock.

Goblins loved to cause terror in the darkness, and they took special glee when the father in a home passed away. The spirits waited. Then in the dead of night, they attacked. They zipped through the air just above the beds. They pounded on walls. They yanked off covers. When children trembled, the beings snorted with fiendish joy. Even babies did not escape their meanness. Goblins were said to poke and tickle infants to make them cry. With supernatural might, a goblin would press on a sleeper's chest until dreadful visions arose. The creatures also wove cobwebs into nightmares and pushed them into the ears of dreamers.

GOBLINS AND CHILDREN

Although they were evil, goblins could be charming when they played among children. With their powers to fly and do tricks, they were great fun. Goblins encouraged their human playmates to play pranks and disobey their parents. The spirits then disappeared once the children were caught. The youngsters bore the punishment alone while the creatures laughed. Goblins also liked to hide or break things. Then they watched as one family member blamed another.

Over time the goblins settled down. They grew accustomed to humans and their way of life.

According to legend, once more changes took place in the goblin world.

HOBGOBLINS

Goblins came to enjoy human food, especially fine wines. They liked the warmth of a home with a fireplace. Some goblins became tamer. The English called this improved home spirit a hobgoblin, meaning "goblin of the hob," or side of the fireplace. Hobgoblins were the size of goblins, but their bodies were softer and furrier. Like goblins they could still be wicked, and each one jealously ruled over its own farm or home. Unlike goblins, these spirits chose to be useful at times. Still, they offered their help only if humans followed their rules. A roaring fire had to be left burning at night. Bread, salt, and the best wine, as well as bowls

A hobgoblin removes a pot of stew that was simmering on a family's fireplace so he can enjoy the fire's full warmth.

of hot cereal with cream, were supposed to be placed on the hearth for a midnight meal.

In return the hobgoblin made life easy. House-maids awoke to find the kitchen swept up and water brought in. The chickens laid more eggs, and cows gave more milk. With little churning, cream quickly turned to butter. Fields were easily plowed, and the right amount of rain fell for abundant crops. The hobgoblin tried to protect the health of its people so that they could continue to provide it with a cozy life. If someone was about to die, the being moaned a warning to signal family members to get help. When needed, the hobgoblin stole milk, corn, and even good luck from neighbors to give to its own humans. Some spirits fiddled and danced under the moonlight to entertain their households.

Hobgoblins were also mischievous jokers, however. They pulled pranks on their families and laughed

One goblin swings by the light of the moon while another goblin in the shape of a spider warns him to keep away from his web.

at them. They mixed up salt and sugar and put sand in the flour bin. They rearranged the furniture at night because it amused them when humans got up in the dark and tripped. Hobgoblins especially loved to braid together the tails of two horses or the hair of two sleeping girls. Often the horses' tails and the girls' locks had to be cut off to free them. Another favorite practical joke was to ride the horses all night until the animals were exhausted. At daybreak their owners were furious that the horses were too tired to work.

BAD SPORTS

For all their pranks, hobgoblins were not good sports. Humans were not allowed to laugh at them or get annoyed at their behavior. If people spoke or acted disrespectfully, a hobgoblin quickly repaid the insult. It broke pottery and no longer helped with chores. These spirits were even said to vomit into milk pails and cause cows to produce sour milk. When these creatures got truly angry, their wicked goblin nature came out. Enraged hobgoblins charged and clobbered people so hard the humans passed out. They seized mortals and flew them through the air at heart-stopping speeds. Newborn calves and colts died, and other cattle were thrown over cliffs. Hobgoblins also threw splinters that caused terrible pain in humans and animals.

Goblins and hobgoblins have long been believed to inflict diseases like cramps, sudden dizziness, blackouts, pain in the bones, heart attacks, and heatstroke.

This fearsome hooded goblin was created by special effects artists for the 1988 horror film Phantasm II.

Birth defects, deaths, and accidents were also blamed on the evil beings. To avoid such misfortunes, desperate humans tried to keep the spirits happy.

Still, a goblin never needed a reason to cause distress to humans. Just the existence of people was reason enough. The creatures never forgot that mortals were their enemies. A goblin was most dangerous when it wandered about under cover of darkness, for its sole task was to get revenge on people and to gain power over them.

Goblins

CHAPTER 2

Encounters with Goblins

Goblin folklore from Europe dates back to the Middle Ages, the period from about 500 to 1450. Historians have an idea about how the legends began in Britain. They think the first sightings of mysterious little night people might have been of **Druid** children. The Druids were an ancient religious group. The Romans hated the Druids' beliefs and practices and tried to kill them off. By the first century A.D., most Druids had fled the continent of Europe. Many settled in England and Ireland. But centuries later they were ill-treated there.

Historians think Druids went into hiding in forests and caves and sent their children out at night to steal food from homes and farms. Druids did a wildly excited dance as part of their worship.

A group of Druids dances wildly around Stonehenge in this illustration. Some people believe Druid children were the inspiration behind the first goblin legends.

They also wore green, a color people said they saw on goblins. People might have seen children creeping about at night or dancing in out-of-the-way spots. Such encounters could have started legends about magical creatures like fairies and goblins.

However the tales began, goblins most likely received their name from a story that arose in a French town. Long ago a myth began about a nasty little spirit said to harass people in this town. The residents named the being Gobelin. The modern word *goblin* probably came from this French term. Another English name for the beings was bogeys. The Scottish referred to them as brownies, while Germans named such phantoms kobolds. The fear of these tiny beings with the power to harm humans was almost universal until the latter part of the 19th century.

Goblins

In 1880 Wirt Sikes, a U.S. official who lived in Wales, published a book called *British Goblins*. He interviewed people from all parts of Great Britain. Most individuals insisted that tales of goblins and other little people were fantasies. They maintained, however, that ignorant folks in other regions did believe the old superstitions. Still, wherever Sikes traveled in Europe, especially in Wales, he heard stories from people who claimed to have encountered goblins.

Goblin Tales

Many people said they came upon goblins near a cave in Scotland. Residents of the area named it Goblin's Cave. In North Wales, goblins were said to fly about inside a certain cave. According to legend,

An old ad for a camera known as the Kodak Brownie features a young girl trying to snap a picture of a brownie, as goblins were known in Scotland.

people who went within five steps of the mouth of the cave were drawn in against their will, never to escape. The local peasants stayed far away. It was said that animals feared the spot, and no human could force them near. The grass in front of the cave grew high and thick. Because the cave was hard to see, a pack of hounds once chased a fox right up to the entrance. Suddenly the fox spun around. Its fur stood straight up. Its mouth dripped with froth. In its terror to avoid the goblin cave, the fox ran straight back into the pack of dogs. Still, the hounds would not eat it because a smelly slime covered its fur.

A fiddler once ventured too close to the same cave. Those who watched said that with a whoosh, an eerie mist yanked him inside. He was sometimes seen at night by the front of the cave. While hideous goblins flew about, his fiddle played a strange, sad tune. Yet the fiddler's arms never moved. His face looked as pale as death, and his head dangled loosely about. Later, on a cold Sunday night, the door of a nearby church flew open during a service. The same strange tune ripped through the chapel like a fierce wind. It bounced off the pillars and broke the windows.

TERRIFYING GOBLINS

It was said goblins tried to harm people who attended church services. The **Welsh** claimed the creatures especially disliked the **Methodists**, who drove many goblins away. A tale was told about a goblin from Wales that used its ability to shape-shift

to terrify a minister. It followed the preacher into a field. Then it attacked from behind. When the man turned around, before him stood an exact copy of himself–his person, his dress, even his prayer book. Shocked into speechlessness, the minister escaped on horseback. When he glanced back, the goblin wore a wicked grin from ear to ear.

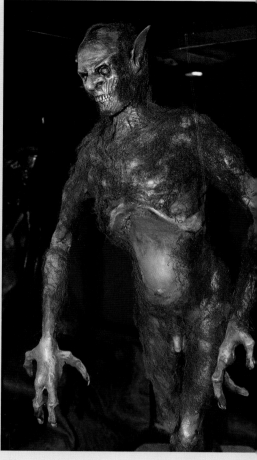

Another shape-shifter story from Wales is the legend of the Dog of Darkness. It tells of a goblin that shape-shifted into a huge phantom with red eyes that flamed. Its scorching breath seared into nothingness any tree or bush in its path. The monster appeared in the moonlight to terrify any mortal it met.

This gruesome wax model is of a goblin who supposedly fed on children's blood during the Middle Ages.

Other goblins became violent to maintain control over their territory. Some strangled new workers who came into their fields. The tale of Leshy warns about a Russian forest goblin. The gigantic Leshy had blue skin, but his eyes, hair, and beard were all green. He hated for humans to enter his forest. It was said he scared lumberjacks and fishermen and got them to go deeper and deeper into the woods. They became lost and too exhausted to walk. Most of them were never seen again.

Like forest goblins, indoor spirits were also protective of their homes. Hobgoblins that lived behind stoves or in cellars were usually connected to the soul of the first owner of the house. The beings stayed even if the owner died or the family moved. The new residents had to adjust. They fared well if they were obedient to the creature.

Goblins were thought to be full-time residents of Welsh mines such as this slate quarry in northern Wales.

The need to be obedient to goblins was well known to miners at the limestone mines in Wales. They claimed the beings did not harass them as long as the men were considerate. Sometimes the goblins were even helpful. At times the miners reported mysterious thumping in the walls of a mine. When workers dug at the spot where the noise came from, they discovered a rich vein of ore. The miners gave the goblins credit for such finds. Yet they also blamed goblins for deadly accidents. They said the spirits caused mishaps because a human laughed at them or spoke impolitely.

Many humans believed their troubles were caused by goblins. Such people followed superstitions to prevent future encounters with the annoying creatures.

Protection Against Goblin Attacks

If the beings were already around, it proved easier to get rid of hobgoblins than to get rid of their more wicked cousins, the goblins. Yet it was commonly accepted that to be good and holy was the best protection against all evil creatures. Mothers warned naughty children that the bogeyman would get them if they did not behave. Some spirits were reported to grow bored with adults who did not lose their tempers while under attack. Soon the beings left. Babies were supposed to be protected from goblins if their mothers remembered to bless them or pray over them at bedtime.

Encounters with Goblins 23

The bogeyman, seen in this illustration hovering over an old woman, has filled the hearts of countless children with fear.

Still, many people took extra precautions. Parents left a knife in the child's cradle to fend off goblins. They sprinkled salt water around the house. People never slept with their heads to the north, which was known to be the land of goblins and death. Others put a coffin nail under the foot of their beds. They knew goblins, like all magical beings, shunned iron.

Goblins

Some humans used trickery to drive the beings away. One story tells how a farmer outsmarted a demanding hobgoblin. In the tale, the creature constantly gave orders to a farmer whose land he lived on. He insisted the farm was his. The spirit's mean temper caused so much trouble that the farmer finally agreed to its demands. They struck a deal. The farmer would do all the work, yet he would give half of his crop to the hobgoblin.

A tiny Japanese goblin with long ears and a pointed nose does a dance on the head of a mushroom.

Before the farmer planted the next crop, he asked the creature if it wanted the tops or the bottoms of the crop. The hobgoblin snarled that it wanted the tops. The farmer planted carrots, and when the crop came in, the hobgoblin received only leaves. Furious, the creature demanded that it wanted the bottoms of the next crop. The following season, the farmer planted wheat. When the hobgoblin realized its share was roots and stubble, it flew into a rage. It left the farm and never came back.

Another way to free a home of a hobgoblin was to put out tiny new clothes. If the being decided the clothes were not fine enough, it had a temper tantrum and left for good. If the clothes were excellent, the hobgoblin felt proud. It went to town to show them off and never returned.

When a hobgoblin became more of a pest than a help, a housewife scattered flaxseed everywhere at bedtime. Not able to tolerate disorder, the creature toiled all night to pick up every piece. Finally the hobgoblin became so disgusted that it went away to find a tidier home. Still, it was risky for humans to drive goblins and hobgoblins out of their homes. According to superstition, bad luck was sure to follow.

For thousands of years, myths about goblins and the troubles they brought have been told and retold in every corner of the world. Although they were based in fantasy, the spellbinding goblin legends inspired storytellers, writers, and poets.

CHAPTER 3

Stars of Stage and Screen

Over the centuries, goblins have appeared in books and poems. In the 20th century, they started to show up in cartoons, movies, TV shows, and video games. These magical beings came from the oral traditions and fairy tales passed from one generation to the next and from great classics of English literature.

In the mid-1590s, William Shakespeare wrote about a hobgoblin named Puck. He serves Oberon, the king of the fairies, in the play *A Midsummer Night's Dream*. Puck causes trouble constantly. He puts spells and charms on the wrong people and enjoys the problems he creates.

Like Puck, the goblins in *The Princess and the Goblin* take pleasure in the harm they cause people.

The mischievous hobgoblin Puck dances gleefully in this illustration of a scene from Shakespeare's play A Midsummer Night's Dream.

In this book, written by George MacDonald in 1872, the creatures plot revenge against the princess and other mortals. The goblins hate the humans who live where they once lived and who mine near their underground homes. The clever creatures are strong except in their soft, toeless feet. They have hideous, misshapen bodies and faces.

Little Orfant Annie by James Whitcomb Riley continues the idea of goblins that terrorize for a reason. In the famous poem, the frightful beings punish naughty children. The housemaid, Annie, warns children they must mind their parents, do their chores, and give to the poor. She says they are in danger if they do not obey, telling them:

> . . . An' the Gobble-uns gits 'at you
>> Ef you
>> Don't
>> Watch
>> Out!

In two popular series of books, goblins are out to get anyone in their way. They are monstrous fighters in *The Chronicles of Narnia: The Lion, the Witch, and the Wardrobe* by C.S. Lewis. Goblins are just as cruel in *The Hobbit* and the three books in *The Lord of the Rings* series by J.R.R. Tolkien. As a child, Tolkien loved *The Princess and the Goblin.* The gruesome goblins he created are similar to those from the princess tale. In *The Hobbit,* Tolkien named his creatures goblins, but in *The Lord of the Rings,* he made the same beings smaller and renamed them orcs. Orcs have glowing eyes and oversize pointed ears. They have snoutlike noses and fangs. They stand hunched over on bowed legs. When they are injured, their rough, bumpy skin sheds black blood. They are miserable beings inside and out and exist only to cause destruction.

In the *Harry Potter* book series, goblins are shriveled creatures that fiercely guard the bank they manage. These smart goblins, who speak a language called Gobbledygook, have deep-set eyes, pointed ears, hooked noses, and long fingers. They are greedy characters who turn threatening when someone cannot pay back a loan of money. More than once these goblins violently revolt against the wizards that oppress them.

ON THE SCREEN

Stories from *Harry Potter, The Chronicles of Narnia,* and *The Lord of the Rings* were all turned into successful movies. Another movie featuring a goblin was the 1985 animated film *The Black Cauldron.* In this movie, a boy named Taran and his odd friends race to find a magic item that will give ultimate power to its owner. They fear the wicked Horned King might gain it. The goblin, Creeper, is the clumsy leader of the Horned King's henchmen. He has bulging eyes and sharp features.

Actress Jennifer Connelly appears alongside the goblin Hoggle in Jim Henson's 1986 movie Labyrinth.

Dressed in armor and wielding weapons, these unsightly goblins are ready for battle in a scene from the 2005 movie The Chronicles of Narnia.

Goblins are a major force in *Labyrinth* a 1986 movie directed by Muppet creator Jim Henson. Jennifer Connelly plays a teenage girl named Sarah. Sarah battles against time to rescue her baby brother from the Goblin King, a powerful sorcerer played by David Bowie. Although the goblins unite to stop her, Sarah finds her way through the magical labyrinth of Goblin City. Some of the goblins look like shrunken men the size of children.

Some look like birds that stand on four legs. The creatures have various colors of skin, and many are hairy. Most have warty, leathery skin and wide mouths with rotten teeth or fangs. Hoggle, the main goblin, looks as mean and sneaky as the others, but he becomes Sarah's friend.

David Bowie appears in his crazy labyrinth as the evil Goblin King in a scene from Labyrinth.

Goblins

On the small screen, another modern girl battles demons and goblins in the animated television feature *The Inuyasha Show,* on the Cartoon Network. In the program, which first aired in 2002, Kagome enters the world of Japan long ago and must protect a prize jewel in her possession.

HOLLYWOOD'S MOST FAMOUS GOBLIN

The most famous goblin in pop culture is the Green Goblin. He first appeared in the *Amazing Spider-Man,* the Marvel comic book created in 1964 by Stan Lee and Steve Ditko. The Green Goblin, Spider-Man's arch enemy, is actually a deformed man named Norman Osborn. Before green fluid exploded in his face, Osborn was a gifted scientist. The accident caused him to go crazy. It also made him as strong as Spider-Man. Osborn begins to dress in a goblin costume that has freakish eyes. As the Green Goblin, he is determined to kill Spider-Man and take over as the leader of the city's criminals. He invents the Goblin Glider, a personal flying gadget, and pumpkin-shaped, handheld exploding weapons. He also makes throwing missiles called Razor-Bats and gloves that fire blasts from the fingertips.

Another comic-book villain is the Hobgoblin, who takes on an identity similar to the Green Goblin to battle Spider-Man. In the beginning, the Hobgoblin possesses no special powers. Then, as his evil deeds grow, he gains supernatural abilities.

The scary Green Goblin jets across the Manhattan skyline in this still shot from the 2002 blockbuster movie Spider-Man.

The Green Goblin first appeared on television when the animated series *Spider-Man* aired in 1967. Some fans complained that the TV creature was not true to the comic-book goblin: The original character had relied on inventions to commit crimes, but the TV Green Goblin focused on magic. In the 1980s TV series, the character changed even more. He no longer had control over himself when his form changed from human to goblin.

Played by Willem Dafoe, the Green Goblin became a famous character in the 2002 film *Spider-Man* and its 2003 sequel, *Spider-Man 2*. In these movies, his goal is still to

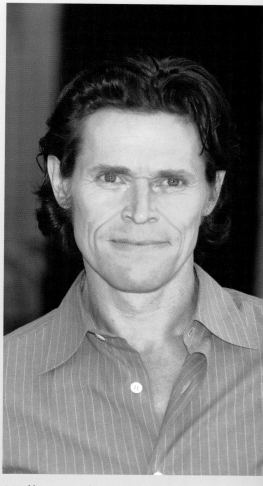

Willem Dafoe is the actor who played the Green Goblin in the Spider-Man *movie series.*

defeat Spider-Man. He evolves into the Ultimate Green Goblin, who has such superhuman strength that bullets bounce off his skin. The creature is a murderous, insane monster that causes the death and suffering of many people.

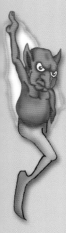

GAMES AND TOYS

Goblins that are purely evil, like the Green Goblin, appear in popular video games. Partly wicked ones are featured, too. The older, absolutely mean type of goblin is usually somewhat frail. These goblins have different colors of skin and grimy, tangled hair. This species of goblin appears in the game *Dungeons & Dragons* and belongs to a goblinoid species along with bugbears, kobolds, and hobgoblins. The corrupt, but not totally evil, goblins are green and bald. They show up in the game *Warhammer* and in the *Warcraft* series of games. In addition there are many subgroups, including ancient forest goblins and weird night spirits.

In most games, goblins are brutal characters that constantly cause wars. As small creatures, they stay alive through cleverness instead of strength. Yet in the *Palladium Fantasy Role-Playing Game,* goblins depend on group strength to survive. Most of them serve as common soldiers, thieves, and spies and blindly follow the most powerful goblins in their tribes. Only the Cobblers have kept the old magic. They are held in great respect by the common goblins, who are dumb.

A brainy race of green-skinned goblins appears in the *Warcraft* games. They have different jobs. Some goblins protect gold mines in the forest, but many of them build engines and machines. They

especially like steam machinery and things that blow up or make noise. Goblins compete against the gnomes to build the best equipment. In contrast, the goblins in *Final Fantasy* are imps, the weakest spirits. These brown-skinned creatures have huge round noses and large eyes. Although they look harmless, one of their favorite foods is brains.

The goblins in the *Gobliiins!* series appear comical. They have cartoonlike eyes and long ears and noses. Some have tails and odd horns.

A screen shot from the Warcraft *game series includes a stylized goblin warrior.*

Goblins

These creatures use their abilities to do magic, hit hard, and operate objects in funny ways.

Goblins in the collectible trading card game *Magic: The Gathering* are also humorous beings. They love rocks. Their word for flying actually means "falling slowly," and they have 42 different words for *ouch*. They are considered smart if they can do two things—hit and run. If they are clever enough to figure out which end of a spear is sharp, they get promoted to guard duty.

Pop Culture Goblins

Goblins of every kind—evil, clever, silly, and stupid—continue to be a part of pop culture. Dolls and play figures are modeled on the characters in movies, TV shows, and games. Construction sets with superhero figures allow fans to build scenes based on stories from movies, comic books, and TV shows. There are goblin beach towels, collectible cards, posters, art, and even hand-size goblin figures that function as walkie talkies. The image of goblins today is just as varied as it was in ancient stories. Some are hoaxsters. Some are even helpers and some are horrors.

The frightful goblin most Americans encounter each year is the kind found only at Halloween. These creatures—who appear in ghastly

Countless dolls and play figures have been designed after the distinct goblin characteristics.

This Green Goblin toy is just one of many goblin-themed toys and games available to consumers.

costumes and monstrous masks—shout, "Trick or treat!" Like those who left out treats to please their hobgoblins, people today give the goblins at their doors candy. Like folks in centuries past, modern-day people cannot rid the world of goblins.

Glossary

Celtic: Pertaining to the ancient customs and languages of western and central Europe, especially Ireland, England, Scotland, Wales, and northwest France.

Druid: A member of a pre-Christian religion in Rome, Britain, and Ireland.

gnome: One of a race of small beings that live inside Earth and guard its treasures.

grotesque: Fantastically ugly, odd, or unnatural in shape, appearance, or character.

Methodists: Members of a large Christian group.

mortals: Humans; beings who will die after a normal life span.

revenge: Punishment or injury to another for a wrong done to oneself.

shape-shift: Change appearance from one form into another.

superstitions: Beliefs or fears not based on reason or knowledge.

territory: A place or area that someone claims as his or her own.

unearthly: Supernatural; something that does not belong to Earth or this world.

Welsh: Pertaining to the country of Wales, its people, or their language.

FOR FURTHER EXPLORATION

BOOKS

Anna Franklin, *The Illustrated Encyclopedia of Fairies.* New York: Sterling, 2005. This book explains ancient folklore traditions from all over the world. It provides definitions of 3,000 fairy beings such as goblins, giants, ghouls, ogres, elves, tiny winged sprites, brownies, and tree spirits. It also has beautiful illustrations.

Carol Rose, *Giants, Monsters, and Dragons: An Encyclopedia of Folklore, Legend, and Myth.* New York: W.W. Norton, 2001. This book describes giants, monsters, dragons, and mystery animals and tells about their behavior and origins, as well as the culture and time they came from.

Carol Rose, *Spirits, Fairies, Leprechauns, and Goblins: An Encyclopedia.* New York: W.W. Norton, 1998. This entertaining book features the antics of 2,000 beings such as angels, elves, fairies, familiars, keremets, nats, nymphs, and other strange creatures from all corners of the world.

WEB SITES

British Goblins, Welsh Folk-Lore, Fairy Mythology, Legends and Traditions (www. sacred-texts.com/neu/celt/wfl). This Web site provides the text of the book written by Wirt Sikes in 1880.

James Whitcomb Riley Web site (www.james whitcombriley.com/children%27s_poetry.htm). This Web site features Riley's children's poetry, including *Little Orphant Annie* and *Nine Little Goblins*.

Magical Creatures (www.kidsdomain.com/kids/ wizard/creatures.html). This Web site explains the differences among magical creatures that appear in classical stories and Greek legends. It tells how a goblin differs from a golem. It also lists stories that feature unicorns, trolls, mermaids, dragons, and fairies.

INDEX

PICTURE CREDITS

About the Author

Jennifer Guess McKerley has written other nonfiction books for children and has published articles in magazines and newspapers. She likes to travel and spend time with her husband and two children. Her hobbies are reading, solving word and number puzzles, and walking in the mountains.

611